Grandma Mary—
Her True Stories

Text and songs by Mary Halter
Illustrated by Anne Halter
Also available in audio tape and CD

CONTENTS

THE CATS AND THE MOUSE

We once had a mother cat who was a calico cat. She was orange and white, black and tiger colors all over. She had three kittens right in the middle of our living room floor. What a surprise they were: one was gray; one was white; and one was creamy orange. We named the gray one, Muffy; the white one, Tuffy; and the creamy orange one, Taffy. Tuffy was white at first; but then his ears, his paws, his nose, and the tip of his tail began to grow darker in color as he grew older. What do you suppose he turned into? He turned into a Siamese cat. Imagine that! A Siamese cat from a calico mother.

We kept Taffy and Tuffy as part of our family and we enjoyed them very much. On one winter day when the cats were about six months old, I found them in the kitchen with a mouse. The mouse was lying on its side, and I thought it surely must be dead. One of our daughters picked it up and put it in a shoe box, and then put the box on a high shelf near the back door. We were going to put the mouse outside later. But when I went back later and looked in the box, the mouse was gone. Well, it wasn't dead after all! It must have jumped out of the box.

A few days later, the same thing happened again. Taffy and Tuffy were batting the mouse around. Again the mouse just lay there, looking dead. Again we picked it up, and again we put it in the shoe box. But this time, we took the box out to the garage and left it there. If the mouse was still alive, it could survive on the sunflower bird seed that was out there.

That night, it snowed quite a bit—more than six inches. When I went outdoors the next day, what did I see in the snow but little, tiny mouse footprints, leading from the garage to the back door of our house. That was up three big steps, too. And I didn't see any footprints leading away from the door. It looked like the mouse had walked right back into our home. When I went inside, I called out to the mouse: "O.K., mouse, I saved you twice, and still you came back. Now, you're on your own."

And do you know what? I never did see that mouse again. Here is my song for the cats and the mouse:

> The mouse, the mouse, the mouse
> Came into the house, you see.
> I don't know why that mouse so fair
> Would want to come back into a house where
> Two fine cats lay waiting.

THE FURRY CRITTER

As I was walking by the river one day,
I heard a new sound I'd never heard before.
I thought it was a bird, but nowhere did I see
Any sign of any bird up there in any tree.
Then I thought to myself: it sounds like it's coming
    from below.
So I looked down at the ground. And what do you
    know?
There was a little furry critter staring up at me.
There he sat only a few inches from my feet.
I sure hadn't expected a furry critter to meet.
The critter blinked his eyes. I'm sure he
    wondered what he saw.
I blinked my eyes, too, because what he saw was
    ME!
As I studied his fur, I came to realize—
This was a baby raccoon sitting right before my
    eyes.
And one thing is certain: when there's a baby
    raccoon—
        A mother is near!

        I'm getting out of here!

THE SAD RABBIT

We have had several pet rabbits at our home. Binky was one of our first rabbits; then there was Mother Rabbit, Snuffy and Peter Rabbit. Then when our son, Tom, was about fourteen, he brought home another rabbit. We'll call him Andy for short. Andy was a dwarf chocolate and white, Dutch-belted rabbit. Tom put him in a fish aquarium in his upstairs bedroom. But Andy, though a dwarf rabbit, soon outgrew that home. So I let Andy have our upstairs powder room for his house. We have found that rabbits in a home like to chew on electrical cords, curtains, and sofas. The bathroom was ceramic-tiled and had almost nothing for a rabbit to chew on. One of Andy's favorite pastimes was to shred up toilet paper and to put it in all corners of the small room. How he loved holding it in his mouth and running it in its place! We had a cat litter box filled with cedar shavings for the rabbit to use, and he did use it most of the time. Tom would bring food and water to Andy, and occasionally clean the room. The rabbit knew Tom the best, and would let Tom hold and pet him.

When Tom went away to college, I faithfully brought food and water to Andy, but I also cleaned up the bathroom a lot. Andy had an old towel which he would lie on in one corner; but I did take away much of the shredded toilet paper. And I patted his head every now and then, too.

One evening, about one and one-half months after Tom went away to school, I went upstairs with food for the rabbit. When I looked at Andy, he looked really sick. He hung his head down and lay down on his side—things he had never done before. I was worried about him and called up Tom at college. He wasn't home then; but when he called back, I told him of my concern, and that I wasn't sure if Andy was going to live through the night. I suggested that Tom send Andy some thoughts of love, and talk to him on the cordless phone which I could bring to the bathroom.

Well—when Andy heard Tom's voice, his ears just perked right up. I tried to do something for the rabbit, too. I massaged his little body, and told him I was really sorry that I hadn't been more considerate of his needs. I gave him lots of toilet paper to shred, and I let him hop around in the hall next to the bathroom.

The next morning, I rushed upstairs to see if Andy had made it through the night. I was relieved and happy to see him alive. Tom came home that week-end to give Andy a little attention and cuddling, too. After that, I tried to pet him and talk to him and rub noses with him often. We all made it through that crisis and learned a lesson, too. Though the shredded paper looked like a mess to me, it looked like home to Andy. When attention from one person is gone, it needs to be replaced from another source. When we choose to share our lives with animals as pets, we have to make a commitment to care for them as long as they live. Andy did live another two years; and I think of him every time I am on that bathroom, now neat and clean. There's a song for Andy, too:

Tom, Tom, the harper's son.
He had a rabbit that liked to run.
And how that rabbit liked to play—
Till Tom went to college eighty miles away.
Who would have thought that a rabbit could be
So very sad it was plain to see
That we had to do something very quick;
'Cause the rabbit sure did look very sick.
So we called up Tom on the telephone,
Saying, "Tom, we need your aid.
You've got to talk to your furry friend,
And tell him he's still your
            funny...
                  bunny...
                        honey!"

THE BUGS IN MY HOUSE

This song is dedicated to some other creatures who share
our earth with us:
   There are many bugs who live in my house.
   Centipedes and spiders live in my house.
   There have even been some fleas in my house.
   Do you know why they've all chosen my house?
   They have heard a rumor that in my house,
   They are very safe there, and it's true.
   Once there was a cricket came in my house.
   Walked right in the door that leads to my house.
   I said, "Cricket, dear, you're safe in my house.
   But you'll have a better life if you're not in my
      house."
   In the middle of the night that cricket came
      creeping.
   Walked across my arm as I lay on the floor
      sleeping.
   I must have felt those cricket feet, for I suddenly
      awakened.
   I opened up the door and let the cricket hop free.
   There are many bugs who live in my house.
   Centipedes and spiders live in my house.
   There have even been some fleas in my house.
   Do you know why they've all chosen my house?
   They have heard a rumor that in my house,
   They are very safe there and it's true.

THE FOX AND THE DUCKLINGS

One June morning, as I walked by the river, I stopped to see if anything was happening there that day. Oh no— nothing seemed to be happening. To my right— upstream—was a pile of rocks; to my left, another pile. Soon some of the upstream rocks started to move. Well! They weren't rocks at all, but a mother duck and seven ducklings. These ducklings looked about half-grown to adult size. When they saw me watching them, they started to swim downstream. They stopped along the other pile of rocks to munch whatever food they found there. Two of the ducklings stayed close to their mother; but the other five swam further along downstream, munching all the way. When the five had reached a certain distance, mother clucked softly to the near-by two ducklings; and the three of them closed the gap.

At the same time, another mother duck and nine very tiny ducklings had come around the bend of the river, and had climbed up a land bank. They were all preening their feathers—even the wobbly little ones. I wondered how the two groups of ducks would interact as they got closer to each other. Did each group have its own territory? Would the mothers communicate with each other? As I watched, the two groups always stayed several feet apart, never intermingling ducklings. The mother ducks kept clucking softly at their own young.

Suddenly the clucking grew louder and louder. I looked around. Padding softly along the same side of the river bank on which I sat was a red fox, and it was looking at the older ducklings only a few feet away. The ducklings had been nearly invisible among the rocks, but the fox's reddish-brown coat color was a sharp contrast to the gray soil behind him or her. I shivered as I watched the fox walk to the middle of the stream, toward the older ducklings. The quacking grew louder. Both mother ducks were quacking and flapping their wings. It seemed that the older ducklings were quacking, too. But it all happened so quickly that I couldn't sort out all of the sounds. I do know that the fox was very silent!

Although I appreciate the balance of nature, and the role of all creatures in it, I did feel the need to respond to what I was seeing. I clapped my hands and called out at the fox. He or she was startled; looked my way briefly; crossed the stream and ran into the brush on the opposite bank. The mother ducks were flapping their wings continuously, and both flew into the air to chase the fox. Then they both came back and settled in quietly with their young again.

Right after the commotion with the fox, a couple of the older ducklings must have come too close to the younger ones; and the little ones' mother chased them away. She chased one in a big circle back to its own mother. As that duckling came "home," one of its siblings swam over to it, and started hitting it with its bill. The two continued this bill fencing briefly until mother swam over, separated the two, and clucked at then both. Then she proceeded to look squarely in the eyes of the duckling who had gotten too close to the other mother, and gave it a few clucks in private. That duckling tucked its head down lower in its neck and listened. I laughed when I saw that behavior. As the mother of six children and a grandmother, too, I have a special appreciation for parents of any species.

Then it was time to walk home—even though I wanted to watch more. Can you guess what I did every time I came back to the river that year? That's right! I counted ducklings!

Here is my song for the fox and the ducklings from the point of view of the mother ducks:

Oh, no fox, not my ducklings—
Even though your hunger's keen.
I will chase you far from here, fox—
So my ducklings can't be seen.

THE LITTLEST GOSLING

Todd Wehr Nature Center is a beautiful part of one of my favorite parks in Wisconsin. I love to search there for special pictures and special experiences. I'd like to share one of them with you. I call the story, "The Littlest Gosling Fights Back."

Canada geese are frequent visitors in our state. They migrate north in summer, south in winter; and sometimes they stay if they find food and open water. They often raise their young ones—called goslings—right near our city.

One goose family that I was watching one spring day had eight goslings. All of them were about the same size— except one. It was much smaller that the rest. It probably hatched from its egg several days after the others. Its siblings were all pecking at it with their bills. When this goose family stood up and marched forward to join a larger group of geese, the littlest gosling was the last one in line. As I watched them, I saw that little gosling go forward and grab the tail of the gosling in front of it with its bill. I think the littlest gosling might have written this song:

You may be older, my brother, my sister.
You may be older, brother, sister, dear.
But older's not better, my dearest, my darling.
Older's not better, fellow goslings hear.

You may be bigger, my brother, my sister.
You may be bigger, brother, sister, dear.
But bigger's not better, my dearest, my darling.
Bigger's not better, fellow goslings, hear.

You may be faster, my brother, my sister.
You may be faster, brother, sister, dear.
But faster's not better, my dearest, my darling.
Faster's not better, fellow goslings hear.

For I am a gosling, a gosling I am.
For I am a gosling, gosling so true.
Though younger, though smaller, perhaps even slow.
But I have gosling rights, I want you to know.

THE LITTLE RED FOX

Several times I have happened to meet a little red fox. She was searching for food—perhaps mice or gophers—on a big grassy field near the river. I was so surprised to see her—she just stared at me and didn't run away. And here's a song for our little fox:

Little fox, little fox, there's the little fox.
She's out there searching for her dinner today.
With her two pointy ears and her bushy tail,
And she doesn't even run away.
No, she doesn't even run away.

Little fox, little fox, how's that little fox?
What has she found for her dinner today?
With her two pointy ears and her bushy tail,
I wonder why she doesn't run away.
No, she doesn't even run away.

THE WHITE-THROATED SPARROW

Beautiful spring days are perfect for listening for bird songs. One year I heard a new bird song, one I'd never heard before. I searched the bare limbs of the nearby trees; and finally located a plain brown bird with no particular feather markings to help identify it—only a beautiful song. I hummed the bird song all the way home, and then worked out the notes on the piano. I worked the bird song into my own song.

All summer I kept listening for the song again. Finally I did hear it again, when I was with some bird watchers. Would someone there know the answer to my question? I was happy to find someone who told me that this lovely song came from a white-throated sparrow. The song has no words to add here, but you can hear my song on the tape-recorded version of these stories.

THE CLEVER HERON

A small town nearby has the name of Oconomowoc, Wisconsin; and it is close to beautiful lakes. Where there are lakes, there will always be many birds and animals. Again this story happened in spring.

I was walking near a big lake one day when a large bird flew low over the highway, and then flew down under the bridge that crossed a river. I could hardly wait to get close enough to see what the bird was—and what it was doing. How I enjoyed what I finally saw! As I searched the area under the bridge, I spotted the bird. It was a Great Blue Heron, and it was standing at the bottom of a waterfall. As I thought about it, I figured out what he was doing. My song will tell you the rest of the story:

> Mr. Heron, how's the fishing?
> How's the fishing out there today?
> I think that it is pretty smart
> To stand at the bottom of a waterfall,
> And wait right there for a fishy treat
> To come tumbling right down at your feet.

Mr. Heron, how's the fishing?
How many fishes do you like to eat?
I think that it is pretty smart
To stand at the bottom of a waterfall,
And wait right there for a fishy treat
To come tumbling right down at your feet.

Mr. Heron, how's the fishing?
How many fishes came tumbling down?
I think that it is pretty smart
To stand at the bottom of a waterfall
And wait right there for a fishy treat
To come tumbling right down at your feet.

Mr. Heron, how's the fishing?
How's the fishing out there today.

DUDLEY, THE POT-BELLIED PIG

The recording studio that I use is in a rural area of Wisconsin. There Don and his family have dogs and cats, goats and rabbits—and a pot-bellied pig named Dudley. The day I met Dudley, he showed me how he can roll over. Pretty clever, isn't he? He loves to have his belly scratched.

Don told me about another trick, too. Just from watching people, Dudley figured out how to open up the refrigerator door and get some apples from the drawer in it. He doesn't close the drawer after himself, though.

I read that pigs can outperform dogs on tricks, and that they have intelligence equal to that of dolphins and chimpanzees.

Well, Dudley, my friend, you certainly taught me something—to appreciate pigs a lot more than I ever did before. I thought such a smart pig surely deserved a song of his very own:

There's a pot-bellied pig named Dudley—
With a funny black, wrinkled-up nose.
This pig has a trick he'll show you.
Would you like to see how it goes?

This black pig can roll right over—
Sure a funny sight to see!
Will you scratch his belly for him?
Make him smile for me.

There's a pot-bellied pig named Dudley—
With a funny black, wrinkled-up nose.
What kind of world is this where pigs do tricks?
Perhaps he could teach us some, too.

MY LOVE SONG

I have written a song:

      for rabbits and birds;
      for foxes, kittens and mice;
      for ducklings of all sizes;
      for flowers, for rivers and for trees;
      for stars, for moon and sun;
      for all the people on the earth;
      for all that is—seen and unseen—

      This is my love song!

www.ingramcontent.com/pod-product-compliance
Lightning Source LLC
Chambersburg PA
CBHW041221040426
42443CB00002B/41